HELP YOUR CHILD TO READ

by

WILLIAM BEET

MALVERN PUBLISHING COMPANY
LIMITED

Published by

Malvern Publishing Company Limited
P.O. Box 16
Malvern
Worcestershire
WR14 1UH
England

ISBN 0-947993-23-1

Printed and bound in Great Britain by
EntaPrint Ltd., Cranleigh, Surrey.

CHAPTER ONE

SHOULD PARENTS TEACH?

The Pre-school child

'I don't know what to do for the best', said John's mother. 'He's only four years old, but he wants to read. The local education authority won't let him start school until the first term after his fifth birthday. That seems ages! Do you think I ought to teach him?'

'Why not?' I replied. 'I think it's wrong to hold back a child, if he's keen and ready to learn. Reading can be such fun!'

'Don't you think that the teachers might object?' asked John's mother.

I assured her that most teachers would be glad to find that a new pupil could already read. My first teaching job had been in a junior mixed and infant school. I knew how pleased my colleagues were when they found that new entrants were keen and fluent readers.

Of course, those teachers who disapprove of teaching by parents may have sensible reasons. So much depends on the common-sense of the parent. If pressure is put on the child, he or she may develop a dislike for reading. If the parent's approach or methods are unwise, the child may become confused and demoralised.

Fortunately many teachers welcome parental help and are willing to advise parents. The Head teacher of the local infant or nursery school may be pleased to talk to parents of pre-school children about pre-reading activities and about the introduction of printed words and letters.

The teacher of a reception class of thirty infants has her hands more than full! If pupils can already read, the teacher's task is made much easier. After all, communication and reading skills are the foundation on which a child's educational progress depends!

The infant school child

'Sheila seems to spend most of her time at school just playing about. She's nearly six years old, and still cannot read. Ought I to teach her?'

Tact is the key word!

This parent was walking on a minefield! The way in which she phrased the question showed that she was critical of the school. She needed to go to the school and tactfully discuss Sheila's apparent lack of progress with the teacher. Tact is the key word! A teacher may feel very vulnerable, and may be very sensitive to criticism, direct or implied. Friendly co-operation between home and school is what is needed!

Of course, there are *some* incompetent teachers, just as there are some neurotic, pushy parents. However, there might have been good reasons why Sheila could not read. Much would depend on her stage of development. Children develop at different rates. Some can read by the age of four. Others develop more slowly, and may not be ready to start reading until much later. That is why you will not find ages stated for the different activities mentioned in this book.

Was Sheila wasting her time 'just playing about'? That would depend on the nature of the play. What appears to the parent to be pointless play may in fact be a valuable way of developing a child's vocabulary and understanding of ideas.

Children can learn a lot from play, whether it is in the school or at home. No child learns to read by reading only in school!

Children can learn a lot from play!

A majority of primary schools now seek to involve parents in the child's education. They realise that the professional training of the teacher, and the special, unique knowledge possessed by the parent can reinforce each other.

As a parent, you almost certainly have a good knowledge of your child's likes and dislikes! You may be able to suggest books and activities which will interest him or her. Many pupils have been put off reading by having fairies stuffed down their throats! They might have responded differently to topics which interested them.

... fairies stuffed down their throats!

The parent has certain advantages over the teacher. He or she can probably give the child undivided attention, unlike the teacher! In addition the parent has an intimate knowledge of the child, a knowledge not possessed by the teacher.

The child who enjoys a warm, relaxed and loving relationship with the parents may make very good progress. Of course, it's important to avoid nagging, and to give the child confidence and fun in a relaxed atmosphere.

Some local education authorities and schools have gone to considerable trouble to involve parents, both at home and in the school. For example, the Inner London Education Authority operate a scheme known as PACT, Parents, Children and Teachers.

9

The nursery or infant school may ask parents to read with their children at home for a short time each evening. The child chooses a book in the class library, and borrows it for a week. The teacher may send a card with the book explaining whether the book is most suitable for reading by the child, by the parent to the child, or by parent and child reading together.

Some Head teachers invite parents into the school to hear children read. One parent volunteer heard thirty different children read during the course of a week! A teacher may have only about one minute per child per day to listen to reading. A parent volunteer may be able to spend half an hour with one child. Child and adult then have plenty of time to talk about what is being read!

If that sort of thing does not happen at your child's school, could you tactfully suggest it? A Head teacher who knows that he or she has the support of parents is unlikely to resent constructive suggestions from individuals or from Parent-Teacher Associations.

For schools and parents contemplating the use of volunteers to assist with the teaching of reading, there is an excellent video-cassette which can be bought for £12. It is available in VHS, or Betamax format, and its title is 'Help a child to read'. Schools or P.T.As can obtain it from Volunteer Reading Help, Centre for Language in Primary Education, Sutherland Street, London, SW1.

Paired Reading

Some schools recommend 'paired reading'. The child and the parent both read aloud at the same time. After reading the book several times with the child, the adult may gradually lower his or her voice and let the child take over.

Some teachers think that the child should be in control and decide when the adult should stop. Others think that the parent should make the decision.

Paired reading may be particularly useful for children who find reading difficult. The method can reduce stress and help to give the child confidence. By the end of the infant school course most children should be able to read independently.

Children with reading problems

About one in every twenty children have severe difficulties in learning to read.

If a parent suspects that the child needs special help, the first step is to consult the Head Teacher. If necessary, the child should then be referred to the local education authority's educational psychologist. In the rare case where there is disagreement between the parent and the Head Teacher, the parent has the right to insist on this.

Further information is given in Chapter Seven, which includes the titles of several books concerned with reading difficulties, dyslexia, etc.

The use of public libraries.

Most public libraries have a large stock of pre-reading picture books and reading books suitable for children in the early stages of reading. The child is able to choose from a much wider range of books than might be available in the school. Most librarians are delighted to give advice and practical help to parents.

Some children prefer non-fiction to fiction. Many don't want anything that looks like a school book. If the child has been in school all day, he or she wants something different. Variety is the spice of life!

The parents' example is important. If the child sees mother and father borrowing and enjoying books, he or she will probably want to do the same.

In 1965 Dr. Joyce Morris carried out research investigating the parental influence on good and poor readers. She found that, in the case of the good readers, 61% of the fathers and 49% of the mothers were members of public libraries. The corresponding figures for parents of poor readers were 15% of fathers and 13% of mothers.

The motto of my teacher training college was 'Practice before precept'.

It's a very appropriate one for parents who wish to encourage their children to read!

CHAPTER TWO
GENERAL PRINCIPLES

Elementary psychology

The first years of a child's life are very important. It is then that good and bad attitudes and patterns of behaviour are established. Many basic skills are learnt most easily during infancy. Difficulties can arise when parents are erratic and inconsistent in their approach to discipline and to teaching.

Some parents can be erratic!

Children can be little monsters! Many will probe to find the limits of acceptable behaviour, if any. They will experiment to find out what they can get away with! They need consistency and a warm, loving but disciplined environment.

Children can be little monsters!

Long before the first day at school the child may have developed a lively, enthusiastic attitude towards learning. Varied activities at home, plenty of conversation, encouragement of imagination and a questioning approach to life, all lay the foundations for subsequent educational progress.

14

Alternatively, if parents are insensitive to the child's feelings and reactions and if they do not provide a stimulating environment, the youngster may become apathetic, uninterested and unco-operative.

Some parents are too demanding and set targets which the child cannot possibly reach. They over-estimate the child's ability, and then blame the school for failure to achieve the required standards. As one disenchanted Head Teacher once said, 'Too many of our parents think that their ugly ducklings are swans.'

It is not easy to form a realistic view of a child's abilities.

Parents may find it harder than teachers because they are so emotionally involved. It is even easier to under-estimate than to over-estimate a child's potential. Many able children are bored stiff because parents and teachers do not realise how intelligent and talented they are.

Unfortunately it is still quite common for pupils to be given school reading books according to their chronological age, and not their reading age. For example, a five year old might be able to read like a typical seven year old, and might have similar interests to a child of that age. In too many of our schools he or she may be given a totally unsuitable, babyish book.

Children need activities suited to their ability and existing level of achievement. Work which is too easy or too hard may cause the child to become bored, frustrated, angry and/or resentful. The boy or girl may develop a hostile attitude towards learning. He or she may become disruptive or, even worse, withdrawn.

May develop a hostile attitude towards learning!

The disruptive child stimulates the parent or teacher to do something about the problem. By contrast, it is very easy to neglect the withdrawn child, and to leave him, sitting alone quietly, doing nothing but not causing any trouble!

Stimulates the teacher to do something!

Of course, not all children who have been given unsuitable work become nuisances or opt out. Some children, who are set work which is too easy, will do it very well. They want to please the adult, and will oblige by doing anything, however silly or babyish it may seem to them.

17

The parent or teacher may think that the child's response is satisfactory, when in fact there is great under-achievement.

If work is too hard or too easy, or if the child is bored, his attention may wander and he may make mistakes.

'Bobby has a grass-hopper brain!' declared his mother. 'He won't concentrate on anything for more than a few seconds.'

It is a fact that children tend to have a shorter span of attention than adults, but I have known some young children concentrate for an hour or more on activities which interested them.

If concentrated thought is involved, it may be unrealistic to expect a typical five year old to pay attention for more than, say, five minutes at a time. By the time he or she is nine, the child may be able to concentrate for, perhaps, fifteen minutes at a time.

If a child does not persevere with a task it may be that the activity does not interest him. The challenge for the parent or teacher is to find an approach or something which does fascinate the child. That's easier said than done!

When setting work, or when helping a child to choose an activity, it is important to make sure that the child has the skills, knowledge and experience necessary for success. For example, when teaching spelling, the parent needs to plan spelling games in such a way that the child will get a high score, say eight out of ten words correct.

Children become discouraged if they experience frequent failure. Imagine the effect of always getting low marks in class, month after month, year after year!

When a child does experience the occasional failure, an encouraging word can help.

'Never mind! Once upon a time I couldn't do that either! We'll try again later. Meanwhile, let's do something different.'

If boredom sets in, or if the child's attention wanders, it may be a good idea to 'ring the changes,' and to introduce a different activity. On the other hand, the child should be encouraged to finish a task successfully, and not to give up at the first sign of difficulty.

It's not always easy to decide on the best course of action. Don't worry about that! Where there is love, a parent can make a lot of wrong decisions without causing any lasting damage.

Ideally the work should be indistinguishable from play.

For pre-school children membership of a playgroup can be very useful, not only to the child but also to the parent. Contact with other people's children gives the parent a better idea of the different stages of development through which the children pass. As I've said before, children do not all reach the same stage at the same age!

Details of play-group associations and recommended books are included in Chapter Seven and in the Appendix.

If a child does not do something when asked, he or she may in effect be saying either 'I can't' or 'I shan't'. It's fairly easy for the parent to find out whether it is a case of 'can't or 'shan't'.

For example, I once set a group of twelve year olds an intelligence test. One girl did very badly. Some weeks later, without divulging the results of their first attempt, I set the test again. I told the group that everyone would receive a prize. The pupil who increased his or her score by the greatest percentage could have first choice of prize. One of the prizes was a book of jokes. The girl wanted it. She increased her score by 16% and won the book! The teachers were amazed. They had always regarded her as being rather dull.

Most people work for some sort of reward. This may be a mother's smile of appreciation, a father's cry of 'Well done!', a feeling of achievement, a feeling of power, someone's gratitude, wages, or pocket money, etc. In the girl's case the reward was a book of jokes! I leave it to the reader to decide when a reward becomes a bribe, and whether some sorts of reward should not be offered to the child.

Some children, like some adults, are 'gifted' psychologists. Some are skilled in manipulating their parents, and may resist attempts to teach them. A subtle approach is needed.

For example, if the parent wants to introduce a three year old to a pre-reading picture book, it may be best to let the child 'discover' it, rather than to thrust it at him. The book can be left in a conspicuous place with its attractive, colourful cover in full view. When the child picks it up, he may take it to the parent and want to talk about it. It's *his* idea!

Parent and child can get a lot of pleasure looking at, and talking about, books together. Older brothers and sisters can help if there is a good relationship between the children. They can read aloud to the younger child and play suitable games together.

Most children do best when they are given plenty of encouragement. It is important that praise should be genuine and well-deserved. A child who has *not* done his best knows it! He will feel only contempt towards the adult who says 'Well done!' when in fact he made little effort.

Non-verbal communication is important. Looks can't kill, but they can cause great distress. Without uttering a sound a disappointed parent can all too easily transmit a feeling of failure to the child. The parent may not even realise that his or her disappointment is obvious. The child may become over-anxious and desperately unhappy if that sort of thing happens very often. That is one reason why teaching should be avoided at times when the parent is tired, overwrought or anxious about the child's lack of progress.

Non-verbal communication is important!

It can be difficult for a parent to be relaxed and patient when the child makes mistakes. He or she may dishearten the child by correcting every mistake, instead of concentrating on just a few. Such a parent may 'succeed' in teaching the mechanics of reading, but fail to transmit a love of books. A child who is subjected to joyless hours of mechanical exercises may develop a hatred of books and the whole process of reading.

The aim of the parent and teacher must be to make sure not only that the child can read, but that he wants to read and does read.

Our son, long before he could read, imitated us by carefully turning over the pages of books. If his parents found books interesting, it followed that there must be something special about reading!

The Basic Rules

Whether a child is a quick or slow learner, certain basic rules apply to learning at home. It can be fun if:-

(a) praise is used, rather than criticism and punishments.

(b) games, activities and books are carefully chosen so that they are suitable for the child's ability, interests and level of attainment.

(c) plenty of time is allowed for the child to absorb and understand new words, idioms and ideas.

(d) the parents have the imagination and patience to cover the same ground in a variety of interesting ways until the child understands and succeeds.

(e) the child is helped to develop self-confidence and to avoid a feeling of failure.

(f) the parents remember that most young children do not normally concentrate for long periods.

(g) the child is allowed plenty of time for playing with other children and for other forms of relaxation.

CHAPTER THREE
PRE-READING ACTIVITIES

The Early Years

...left it there for most of the day...

The house was in an affluent suburb of Bristol. The baby was well-dressed and well-fed. Every morning the mother put it outside in a pram, and left it there for most of the day. Disadvantaged children are not confined to poverty-stricken inner city areas!

It's surprising how many prosperous, well-educated parents do not appreciate the importance of talking to their babies. It may seem unrewarding to talk to a child who is not yet ready to speak, but a baby learns a lot just by listening to conversation.

At the age of six months most babies begin to babble and to imitate noises. By the age of one year the child will probably make recognisable sounds. By the age of two years he or she will be able to speak a limited number of words.

Learning the mechanics of language involves talking, listening, reading and writing. The teaching of reading needs to be integrated with writing and other language activities.

To make progress the child needs to hear plenty of conversation. He or she is able to understand a large number of words long before speech is possible. The parent can help the child to build a vocabulary by naming and pointing to objects around the house and neighbourhood.

Personally I think that 'baby talk' is best avoided. The parent who says 'Pussy drinkee milkee' causes unnecessary work for the child. There is enough to do, without having to learn incorrect speech.

An exception is the use of nursery rhymes. They have as much to do with the sounds and rhythms of words as with their actual meanings. Young children love rhymes that are, first, fun to hear, and, then, fun to learn, and, finally, fun to read.

"Pussy drinkee milkee"

Mothers and older sisters have always sung songs and rhymes to babies, as, indeed, have some fathers and brothers! The sound of a language initially means more to a baby than its meaning.

If the parent has and can play a guitar or a piano, musical rhymes such as ' Ding Dong Bell' and 'Oranges and Lemons' are particularly exciting to young children.

Later the toddler begins to understand the meanings of the rhymes. If he or she is given a picture book of nursery rhymes, the child will find the book relatively easy to 'read' as the text is already very familiar. If there are attractive pictures next to the text, the individual rhyme will be brought quickly to mind. Having learnt the rhyme, the child will find it easier to point to each word as he or she recites the verse.

Nursery rhymes can be a very good introduction to books!

Before the child is ready to read, simple activities such as playing with jigsaws and watching suitable TV programmes are useful. He or she needs practice in looking for patterns, similarities and differences, as a preparation for the later identification of printed letters, words and phrases.

Many children enjoy playing with constructional toys such as Lego. They don't realise that they are developing the hand-eye co-ordination which is so necessary for using a book or controlling a pencil!

Mothers (and fathers!) can have fun playing games with their children to develop the child's powers of observation.

The game 'I spy with my little eye something beginning with...' encourages careful observation, and also draws the child's attention to the initial sounds of words. For example, the sound 'ch-' occurs in words such as church, chimney, chair, cheese, etc.

Card games such as "Snap" and "Happy Families" can be fun, and assist the child to recognise patterns.

Members of the family may enjoy inventing their own games. A list of firms who will sell educational materials and games to parents is given in the Appendix, but care is needed when deciding what to purchase. It is well worth-while to write to a number of firms for their catalogues to get a good idea of what is available.

Families who decide to make some or all of their own games should have few problems in utilising every-day materials.

Pictures can be cut out from old comics, magazines and Sunday supplements. The child can join in by cutting out and pasting the pictures onto cards. Naturally the parent should supervise carefully the use of scissors - a potentially lethal instrument! It's a good idea to use blunt-ended scissors rather than the sharp-pointed variety.

Two identical or similar packs of cards can be made, and then shuffled separately. The child can than play a variety of games involving matching identical or similar pairs of pictures. Another approach is to sort the pictures into sets or groups, e.g. a set of vehicles (car, bicycle, bus, lorry, etc.)

When introducing card games it can be a good idea to use only a few cards at first. The number of cards can be increased as the child becomes familiar with them. Games involving the matching of similar pictures leads to the matching of similar word-shapes when reading begins.

The idea of a story-line can be developed by separating and shuffling pictures from a story in an old comic. The parent can ask the child, 'Can you make me a story by putting these pictures in order?' This sort of game helps the child to organise thought and language in a logical way. Talking together about what is happening in the pictures is an important part of this activity.

Children can get a lot of pleasure from making up their own stories. Mother or father can print the story and the child can illustrate it. Next day parent and child can 'read' it together from the child's "Own Book."

The Use of Flash Cards

Flash cards can be a dreary, boring experience for the child, or they can be useful when used sensibly and in moderation.

A flash card may have a word, phrase or sentence printed on it. One little girl was only two and a half years old when her parents started to teach her to read. She had always been interested in looking at picture books, and the parents felt sure that she could already read some words herself. The parents made their own flash cards and were surprised at how quickly their daughter assimilated a large reading vocabulary of familiar household objects.

As time passed the little girl learnt to construct her own sentences by arranging cards in order. She had learnt the meanings of verbs ('doing words') by playing action games, illustrating the words in question.

The parents had the good sense not to force their daughter to read when she did not wish to do so, but by the age of four she was reading happily and independently.

In some schools the teacher may hold up a flash card in front of the class and point to each word as she reads it. On subsequent occasions the children join in, and chorus the words as the teacher points to them. Eventually the class will be able to read the words unaided, but may have been bored stiff in the process!

Pre-reading picture books

Before a child is ready to understand print he or she needs to develop a large vocabulary by means of conversation and looking at picture books with adults or older brothers and sisters. In addition the child should be able to speak in complete sentences. For example, he or she should be able to say 'Please may I have a drink?' and not just "Give drink.'

Learning to read is a gradual process. Although many children can read a few words by the age of three, some may not be able to do so until they are say, five or six years old.

The most important aim at the pre-reading stage is to help the child to develop a happy, positive approach towards reading. Books are to be enjoyed! If children are having fun with games and books they will not realise that they are being taught!

Pre-reading books usually contain one picture on each page with a few words of description underneath it. It's important that the picture and the description should be on the same page, so that the parent can point to a word and the corresponding part of the picture at the same time.

The book should be colourful and well-illustrated with large print and plenty of space between the words and lines.

As the parent's finger moves from word to word, the child is introduced to the left-to-right eye movements which are so important in reading. He or she also discovers that the lines of print are read from the top of the page to the bottom.

Soon the child will pretend to read the book for himself, imitating the parent. Often children learn a story by heart before they can actually read it. Eventually the child may really be able to read the story, pointing to each word as he or she does so. The parent can test whether or not the child is actually reading by taking words or phrases out of context.

In addition to using the children's section of the public library, most children enjoy having their own 'library' or collection of books. A large cardboard box can be used for a bookcase.

Value for money.

It's always distressing to see expensive toys and games cast aside by the child after very little use. There is a lot of attractively-packed but over-priced rubbish on sale in the shops!

...attractively packed...over-priced...

Before buying toys, games and kits, I suppose that we need to ask ourselves certain questions. Will the child get many hours of enjoyment from the purchase? Is it suitable for the child's level of development? Will it help the child to acquire new skills? Is it value for money?

CHAPTER FOUR
BEGINNING TO READ

Reading schemes and 'real' books.

There is a lot of disagreement amongst teachers about the teaching of reading. Mrs Betty Root, the President of the United Kingdom Reading Association, speaking at the association's conference in 1985, found it necessary to appeal for tolerance and moderation when discussing reading.

...a new head teacher...burned the books.

She related the story of a new head teacher who burned the books in his school's reading scheme to stop the teachers from using them!

A reading scheme usually includes a variety of carefully graded books and other materials. There may be packs of cards bearing letters, words or pictures for vocabulary work and construction of words and sentences. Often there are workbooks with exercises, puzzles and games to develop comprehension, language and reading skills.

The child may be taught to write by using reading scheme cards and workbooks with examples of letter formation, etc. Cassettes may be provided to develop listening and speaking skills.

In the better schemes there is close collaboration between the authors, publishers and educational researchers. One or more teacher's manuals explain the scheme and give suggestions for its use.

The majority of reading schemes are carefully graded so that the work gradually increases in difficulty. Some are intended to be completed by most children during the first two or three years of their primary school education. Others cover a longer perkod, e.g. from five to twelve years of age, and integrate speaking, listening, writing, reading and comprehension.

The cost makes most of the schemes suitable only for use in schools, unless several parents club together.

A scheme which was designed for parents was the Ladybird Key Words Scheme. That is now being withdrawn, and is being replaced by a new scheme, 'Puddle Lane" by Sheila McCullagh. Preliminary indications are that it will be very popular with parents and children.

Critics of reading schemes argue that reading cannot be taught in a formal, sequenced way any more than speech can. They say that reading is not a series of skills, but that the child learns to read by reading 'real' books.

The critics point out that the limited vocabulary of the early books in a reading scheme can make it very difficult to write interesting stories. They maintain that it is better to let the child choose and read 'real' books, even though he or she may skip or guess at the meanings of many of the words. They suggest that the child will be able to work out the meanings of many new words by looking at the sentence as a whole.

Supporters of reading schemes argue that a *good* reading scheme *does* contain interesting stories. The child is put in a position in which he or she is very unlikely to fail. They say that building children's confidence is just as important as exposing them to good stories.

It can be argued that many of the 'real' books presented as an alternative to reading schemes are far too difficult for some children, particularly slower learners. In addition, even if a scheme is used, it need not follow that the child is prevented from looking at the wealth of stories, poems and information books outside the scheme!

It seems to me that parents and teachers need to be flexible, and to vary their approach according to the circumstances and the needs of the child or children.

It is understandable that some teachers with classes of, say, thirty children of mixed ability feel that they need a structured, carefully planned reading scheme. Much of a teacher's time may be consumed by the demands of slower learners and/or disruptive children.

A teachers time may be consumed by disruptive children!

A good scheme ensures that the child enjoys success. For example, the first stage of a reading scheme might consist of, say, twelve very short books. Children take pride in having read a large number of books! Each book reinforces the child's feeling of achievement.

The methodical approach ensures that the child does not become disheartened or confused by having too many new words introduced at one time. Many children need to see a word repeatedly before they remember it, so certain key words can be used throughout the series of books.

Possibly whether the adult chooses a reading scheme or 'real' books depends on his or her personality. Some people like working to a detailed plan. Others like to make things up as they go along! Fortunately research seems to indicate that the choice of method is much less important than having enthusiasm and a good adult-child relationship.

Parents and children working together can overcome difficulties and achieve both enjoyment and fluency.

Careful choice of books is essential. Many educational publishers colour-code their books to give the child and teacher an idea of the book's level of difficulty. The child needs to read a lot of books at the same level to develop fluency and understanding.

Many children beginning to read find fiction easier than non-fiction. A story-line helps them to make sense of what they are reading. On the other hand, some children are more interested in non-fiction than in fiction!

Introducing words and letters.

Before starting this stage the parent needs to be able to answer 'Yes' to the following questions.

Does the child know the meanings of a lot of words? Can he or she talk in sentences? Does the child enjoy stories and like looking at pre-reading books? Can he or she remember stories and retell them to the parent? Does the child understand simple advice and instructions?

Methods of teaching reading.

Paired or shared reading has already been mentioned.(See Page 11) In addition to the controversy about the relative merits of reading schemes and real books, there are differences of opinion about whether teaching should be based on a 'Look and say' or a phonic approach. Many teachers start with a 'Look and say' approach, and introduce letter sounds later, perhaps when the child has acquired a printed vocabulary of a few hundred words.

The 'Look and Say' method.

Concentrating on the letters of each single word can distract the child's attention from the meaning of the whole sentence, so 'Look and say' reading schemes were developed using short sentences. The teacher encourages the child to look at the shape and appearance of the whole word or sentence, rather than at the individual letters. A difficulty is that many words are very similar in shape and appearance, e.g. 'read' and 'road'.

Sentences in 'Look and say' schemes were carefully selected and graded, but many of the first schemes published were very boring. The restricted vocabulary limited the interest of the books! In addition, critics said that wild guessing was encouraged and that the children did not learn how to spell.

The 'phonic' approach.

Many Victorian readers were of this type. The books concentrated on giving practice in the sounds of letters and combinations of letters. 'The cat sat on the mat. The cat was very fat.'

A criticism of the 'phonic' method is that it can lead to slow, hesitant reading. The child may be so busy analysing each word that he never gets round to understanding the sentence or paragraph as a whole. Reading can become a chore instead of an enjoyable experience.

Much depends on the parent's imaginative approach and on the use of interesting games, riddles, etc.

When introducing letters it is best to emphasise their sounds, rather than their names. For example, the name of the letter 'b' is pronounced like the word 'bee', but the sound of 'b' is spoken as in the word 'bat'. To work out for himself how to say a word the child needs to know the letter sounds.

Some letters have more than one sound, e.g. *a*pple and *a*che, *c*eiling and *c*at, *e*gg and *e*vil, *i*mp and b*i*nd, d*o*g and *o*nly, *u*gly and *u*nique, *y*es and fairy. In such cases it's best to introduce the child to the most common sound first.

Another complication is that some letters change their sounds completely when they are in certain combinations, e.g. ch- as in 'chair', sh- as in 'shed', ph- as in 'physics, etc. When choosing an alphabet book make sure that it gives the sounds of the letters and of common combinations of letters. (Longman's Bangers and Mash ABC Book is one such book, price £4.50)

It is true that over 80% of English words are phonetically based, but the child will need help sometimes. For example, compare the sound of the '-ough' in the words 'tough', 'cough', 'ought' and 'bough'!

When playing phonic games with the child it is obviously best to start with simple words that are easily built up. Later, when the child is reading a book, he or she can often identify difficult words by looking at the rest of the sentence.

For example, a child who did not know that'ou' may be pronounced like the 'ow' in 'cow' might not succeed in identifying the word 'house' by phonic methods. Nevertheless, he or she would probably recognise it in the sentence, 'Tom lived in a big house.'

Often the letter 'e' at the end of a word affects the sound of a preceding vowel. Compare the sounds of the letters in italics in the following pairs, 'h*a*t' and 'h*a*te', 's*i*t' and 's*i*te', 'd*u*n', and 'd*u*ne', 'p*o*p' and 'P*o*pe', and 'l*e*t' and 'repl*e*te'.   In each case the presence of the final 'e' changes the sound of the preceding vowel from the short form to the long form. For the benefit of parents who were brought up on the 'look and say' method, perhaps I ought to mention that the vowels are a,e,i,o and u.   The remaining letters of the alphabet are consonants.

Note that there are usually exceptions to any spelling or pronunciation rule.   For example, compare 'bone', 'done' and 'gone'. Two of the three words do not obey the rule. The long form of 'o' is found in 'bone', but not in the other two words.

There's nothing like a "spot of magic" to enliven the proceedings!

Letter shapes can be cut out of thin card, or can be purchased. The child can use them to build up words. When he or she shows signs of boredom, magnetic letters can be introduced. There's nothing like a 'spot of magic' to enliven the proceedings! An iron or steel surface can make a useful 'blackboard' on which to assemble the magnetic letters into words.

To identify some words a children's dictionary can be useful, but the child will need to learn the order of the letters of the alphabet. He or she can play letter card games which involve putting the cards into the correct sequence.

Don't forget that children learn not only seeing and hearing, but also by feeling and doing. The young child can start by tracing letter shapes with his finger and later with tracing paper and a pencil. He can feel the shapes of cut-out letters, and, as he develops, he can play a variety of games of increasing sophistication.

Which are the best methods?

Most teachers are sensible and pragmatic in their approach. They vary their methods according to the needs and ability of the individual child, as far as classroom conditions permit.

Unfortunately there is little doubt that some children do see reading as a narrow, school-based activity which has little to do with their lives outside school.

A method which succeeds with one child may fail with another. Neither children nor adults are identical in their personalities, abilities, achievements and interests. Some work best in groups. Others prefer to work alone. Some love stories. Others prefer books that give them information. Parents will want to choose the books and methods which suit them and their child. Nevertheless, it is advisable for the parents to seek the advice of the school to which the child goes, or will go.

"Barking at print"...is not much use!

Different approaches may be confusing to the child. Whatever methods are used, it is important to make sure that the child understands what he is reading. 'Barking at print', i.e. pronouncing words correctly without understanding their meaning, is not much use!

CHAPTER FIVE.
AIDS TO READING.

Learning to write.

Learning to write helps the child with the basics of reading and spelling.

Children may begin by tracing letters and words. Some young children have great difficulty in controlling a pencil. At first, a crayon may be used.

Most schools do not teach children to do joined-up (cursive) writing until the second year of the junior school, i.e. age 8+. Different schools may teach different styles of printing and cursive writing. It's a good idea to consult the school to find out what style they use.

Printing and cursive writing both involve muscular control and coordination of hand and eye. Some bright children become infuriated because they can think so much more quickly than they can write. Another child who may become very frustrated is the naturally left-handed boy or girl who is pressurised into writing with the right hand. Right is wrong!

Left to themselves many children will produce progressively smaller and smaller letters. Their efforts may resemble the track left by a drunken spider which has struggled out of a pool of paint. It is probably a good idea to use paper with guidelines about one and a quarter inches apart, although some educationalists would not agree!

...a drunken spider!

Before he or she is taught letter shapes, the child may gain experience by 'writing' or drawing patterns, using a continuous flowing movement. He has to learn to start printing in the right place, and to write horizontally from left to right.

Cards with letter shapes can be purchased, or the parent can make some. Before using a pencil, the child can first trace the shapes of the letters by moving a finger along them. Later he can use tracing paper and crayon or thick pencil before using an HB pencil. Make sure that the pencil is sharp, and not worn down to a stub.

Busy parents may prefer to buy expendable work-books such as the Basic Handwriting Books in the Longman 'Learn at Home'series. (Books 1-4 inc. £1.25 each. Author, Margaret Hooton.)

As usual there are various difficulties for the child to overcome. Each letter of the alphabet may be written as a capital letter or as a lower case letter. In addition they may be written in a variety of ways, which the child needs to know in order to read other people's writing.

When teaching printing, note that most letters can be formed from straight lines and circles. However, some systems of teaching printing and cursive writing are devised so that the transition from one to the other does not involve a drastic change in the way in which the child forms the letters.

Once the child has learnt to print, his reading level is likely to rise rapidly. He will enjoy writing his own stories and illustrating them. As he reads he can find out the meanings of words which are new to him, using a suitable children's dictionary.

There are many suitable dictionaries on the market. For example, the Longman Group publish a Picture Dictionary for 4-6 year-olds, price £4.50, and the Breakthrough Dictionary for 6-8 year-olds, price £5.95. Don't forget that the child needs to know the order of the letters of the alphabet in order to use a dictionary!

Defining the meanings of words is not easy, and the child may need the parents' help. After they have gained confidence, some children may enjoy writing and illustrating their own dictionaries, using words which they have read in their story books or information books.

Fun and games with words.

When planning games for beginners, it's a good idea to choose words derived from the child's everyday activities, e.g. bed, breakfast, house, residence, flat, bungalow, garden, play, work, mother, father, parents, uncle, aunt, television, video-cassette, etc. Another useful source of words is the reading book currently in use.

For slow learners, a lot of repetition with different games but the same words is necessary. Some children don't remember a word until they have seen it perhaps thirty or forty times!

Some of the first words that a child learns to recognise will be those which he or she sees on public notices, on food containers and in television advertisements. The parent can help the child to learn the names of objects around the house by labelling them. A duplicate set of labels can be given to the child for matching..

Matching picture cards with words taken from the child's story books can be an interesting game for some children. The child can be given three or four cards, each bearing a different word, to match with the same number of picture cards. For example, the word 'car' might be matched by the child with a picture of a 'Rolls-Royce.' As the child's vocabulary develops more difficult words can be introduced e.g.'vehicle' could be substituted for 'car'.

...may appeal to the childs' sense of humour...

Soon the child should be able to construct simple sentences by arranging word-cards in the appropriate order. Each card has a single word printed on it, e.g. 'the', 'dog', 'man', 'bit', etc. Sentences such as 'The man bit the dog', may appeal to the child's sense of humour. By choosing appropriate words the adult can make a variety of incongruous sentences possible, and so add a touch of fun to what might otherwise be a rather tedious exercise.

As the number of cards is increased, more sophisticated sentences can be built, e.g. 'How do you make a Maltese cross? Tread on his toes!" (Sorry!)

Games can be used to help the child recognise common combinations of letters, e.g. variations of 'Snap' and "Rummy'. For example, in one form of "Snap', when a card bearing the combination 'th' was exposed in one pack, and the word 'path' appeared on the other, the first child to shout 'Snap!' would win the appropriate pile of cards.

Many suppliers sell games of this type. For example, James Galt & Sons supply Rhyming Snap cards which give useful practice in identifying common patterns of sound.

Older children, perhaps from six years upwards, may enjoy a variety of games based on dictionaries. For example, the child might be asked to find the section of the dictionary containing words beginning with the syllable 'car-'. He or she might then be asked to fill in the missing letters in a puzzle:-

Clue	Answer
1. A house on wheels	car----
2 . A floor-covering	car---
3. A ship's load	car--

Simple crosswords can also be fun and will enrich the child's store of words and ideas.

Some children, e.g. dyslexics, find spelling very difficult. When a child is obviously finding work with printed words to be very hard to do, it is best to seek the advice of a professional person, e.g. a teacher of reading or an educational psychologist who has an interest in reading difficulties.

It is sad that it is still possible to find the occasional teacher who will permit a child to get low scores in spelling tests week after week. Imagine the effect on a child who gets a successsion of marks such as 0 or 1 out of 10!

It is also sad to find some teachers who don't attempt to teach spelling at all! Of course, too much emphasis on spelling can make a child reluctant to write freely and imaginatively, and may discourage him from using any but the most simple words. It is all a matter of balance. Creativity and accurate communication are both important.

CHAPTER SIX

CHOOSING AND BUYING BOOKS

One child's meat is another child's poison.

It's interesting to see how a child's tastes and interests change as he or she gets older. Most young children like nursery rhymes and slap-stick humour. A seven-year-old will probably have broader interests, and may prefer adventure stories, puns, riddles and jokes. Many five-year-olds love to read aloud to the parent or teacher each day, but many seven-year-olds prefer to read silently. However, it is still possible for the parents to discuss each book with the child after he or she has read it. It's easy to find out if the child is reading with understanding, and without 'skipping'.

Children who show no interest in reading may become enthusiastic readers if they are given books about their hobbies or books which provide them with information. A problem here is that such books may be difficult for the beginner to read unaided. Paired reading with father or mother may be the answer.

A football fan may make great efforts to read his club's programmes. A child who is interested in doing simple science experiments will extend his or her vocabulary when reading books about them. The Books of Experiments by Leonard de Vries are a good example of books which can be enjoyed by mother and child playing together. The mother who works through a book of simple science experiments, using everyday household materials, may find that she has transformed the child's attitude to reading.

...simple science experiments, using everyday house hold materials...

One young reluctant reader made very little progress, until he developed an interest in archaeology. Blessed with a sympathetic teacher who guided him and who supplied him with relevant books, the boy made amazing progress. Once considered to be backward and in need of remedial attention, he now expects to obtain a University degree.

When the family visits and explores the local library and bookshops, the parents have a valuable opportunity to find out what sort of books appeal to the child. They can also widen the child's horizons by discreetly drawing his attention to a variety of books.

It's best to let the child read what interests him, and not what the adult thinks he ought to want. Obviously, the reading of semi-literate rubbish should be discouraged, but motivation to read is vital.

Male and female chauvinists' section

Often girls are more enthusiastic readers than boys. A writer of popular science books asserts that this is because women have larger 'language lumps' in their brains than men!

Certainly there do seem to be differences in performance in language-orientated activities when we compare males and females.

If the effects are partly or wholly due to the child's environment, they could be connected with parental attitudes. If mother is the one who reads and enjoys books whilst father busies himself with practical activities, girls may imitate 'Mum', and boys may copy 'Dad'.

Nearly all infant school teachers and most junior school teachers of seven and eight-year-olds are women, so the school may reinforce what has happened in the home. Girls may copy teacher, whilst some boys may come to regard reading as a female pursuit.

Perhaps I should not have written this section. All over the country, mothers may be nagging their husbands, urging them to set a good example to their sons by reading voraciously every available book! I suppose that that is a reasonable request, provided that mother takes an interest in, say, science and mathematics, and so sets her daughters a good example!

"Pasteurised" books.

Many pre-war children's books are criticised because of their outlook on life. Their critics allege that the books transmit racialist and white, middle class attitudes. They complain that stereotyping occurs. Women and girls are portrayed doing domestic duties, whilst men and boys take the initiative and exhibit qualities of leadership.

Some publishers now try to ensure that each book has its quota of children from the ethnic minorities. Father may be shown doing domestic chores, whilst Mother may be a high-flying business executive. Some of the fictional children may be members of single parent families to reflect the position in the real world.

The desire to alter attitudes and to 'pasteurise' books by destroying the germs of racial and other forms of prejudice is understandable, but it can easily become ridiculous. Worse, it can inhibit the author from writing real stories which reflect the world as it really is. However, some parents may want to examine books carefully before purchase to see what assumptions are being transmitted to the reader.

Buying books

There is a huge variety of children's books available in bookshops and children's libraries. Over 3,000 new titles are published each year!

The old adage about not judging wine by the label on the bottle applies to children's books. A glossy cover and attractive illustrations may mask a boring text.

The Centre for Children's Books, The National Book League, 45 East Hill, London, SW18 2QZ, has a Current Collection containing one copy of every children's book published in a two year period. (Tel: 01 870 9055).

The Centre is open from 9.30 am to 5.30 pm, Mondays to Fridays. The Centre also organises Children's Book Week which takes place each year during the first week in October. In addition, exhibitions of children's books can be hired by schools, parents' groups, etc.

The National Library for the Handicapped Child, to be known as the Blyton Handi-Read Centre, contains a reference collection of books, filmstrips, videos, computer programs and other materials of interest to parents and teachers of handicapped children. Details can be obtained by sending a large stamped addressed envelope to Beverley Mathias, The Blyton Handi-Read Centre, Lynton House, Tavistock Square, London, WC1H 9LT.

Many excellent books are produced by educational publishers for sale to schools. These may not appear on the shelves of local bookshops, so that parents may be unaware of their existence.

Some educational publishers will supply catalogues of their books to parents. However, the parent will probably have to order the books which she requires from a retail shop. There may be a delay before the retailer receives the books. As the bookseller's profit margin on school books is only seventeen and a half percent, he may charge, say, an extra twenty five percent to compensate himself for the overheads involved in handling such a small order.

As stated earlier, most reading schemes are too expensive for parents to purchase for use by individual children. An exception may be when parents co-operate to form a pre-school playgroup or nursery class.

A summary of some of the most popular reading schemes is given in the Appendix.

Whether a book is part of a reading scheme or not, most educational publishers state the reading age for which it is intended. An eight year old girl who can read as well as a typical twelve year old is said to have a reading age of twelve years. Conversely, a slower learner might be eight years old, but might have a reading age of only five years!

When a child's reading age is less than his actual (chronological) age, finding suitable books can be a problem. An eight year old does not want to read books intended for five year olds! Fortunately some publishers produce books with simple vocabularies but with story-lines suitable for older children.

Names and addresses of publishers of educational books can be found in publications such as The Education Authorities Directory, the Education Year Book and the Writers' and Artists' Year Book. These may be consulted in the Reference Section of most public libraries. Another source of information which contains reviews of children's books is the Times Educational Supplement. It is published weekly, and can be seen in the reading room of the local public library.

Before buying educational books it is advisable to consult the child's teacher or, in the case of a pre-school child, the Head teacher of the school which he or she will probably attend. Co-operation between home and school is very important. Another point to consider is that the child may become irritated and rebel if he or she has the same books at home as at school.

Cutting costs

Time and money can be saved if several parents co-operate and buy books ands materials on a sharing basis. It is useful if the group includes a qualified teacher to give advice about the suitability of books, etc.

Some schools, particularly schools in affluent areas with strong Parent-Teacher Associations, are well-stocked with books and will let children take books home to read. However, those facilities are not available for the pre-school child, nor for children in schools without adequate financial resources.

Of course, if parents band together to buy books for use in their homes, there can be problems. Disputes can arise over lost, damaged or defaced books. There may be personality clashes. Arguments can occur if several children want to borrow the same book at the same time, or if a book is not returned when due.

CHAPTER SEVEN

SOURCES OF ADVICE FOR PARENTS

Children with reading difficulties

An appreciable number of children experience difficulty when learning to read. Sometimes the difficulty may be due to defective sight or hearing.

In a slim volume such as this it is not possible to give detailed advice, but the nursery or primary school Head Teacher should be able to initiate action where necessary. The names of various organisations concerned with children are given in the Appendix.

All local education authorities operate Child Guidance Units and Remedial Reading Services. Worried parents should first consult the child's Head Teacher.

Most parents will have heard the word 'dyslexia'. It is a word that is often misused to cover any case involving backwardness in reading. Strictly it refers to an abnormality of the brain which makes it difficult for a child or adult to make the necessary connection between speech, print and spelling.

'Do you know what I think? I think that God's put my brain in upside down'.

The words were spoken by a boy, the first of three dyslexic children in one family. The mother has written a book giving practical advice to parents of dyslexic children. It is called 'This book doesn't make sens, cens, sns, scens, sense (Living and learning with dyslexia)', by J. Augur. Published by Better Books, 15a Chelsea Road, Lower Weston, Bath, Avon, it costs £4.95.

Another useful book is 'Dyslexia - a guide for parents, teachers and children' by P.J. Congdon, price £3.00 It can be obtained from the author at 21 Hampton Lane, Solihull, West Midlands, B91 2QJ.

Parents may also find 'Overcoming Dyslexia' by B. Hornsby, price £3.50, published by Martin Dunitz, to be useful.

Those who want to read an academic book which takes a broad view of reading problems in general might like to consult 'Reading difficulties: their diagnosis and correction' by G.L. Bond, 5th edition, price £24.65. published by Prentice Hall. It is mainly intended for classroom teachers.

Recommended reading for all parents

A very wide range of pamphlets and booklets for parents and teachers may be purchased at very reasonable prices from the Reading and Language Information Centre, School of Education, University of Reading, London Road, Reading, RG1 5AQ. They include lists of early readers, stories to read aloud, easy information books, poetry books, etc. Parents can obtain a   current publications order form by sending a S.A.E. to the Centre.

The National Confederation of Parent-Teacher Associations, 43 Stonebridge Road, Northfleet,

Gravesend, Kent, sell a number of publications, including some from the Home and School Council.

Parents with children in the age range 3 - 6 years may be interested in 'Getting Ready for School - a parents' guide', by Margaret Basham, published by Longman, price £2.95. SBN 0 582 25050 1. This sets out to advise parents how they can best prepare their child for the 'vital' early years at school.

Two other books which may be of interest have been published by Allen and Unwin. They are 'The Pre-school Book' by Brenda Thompson, and 'The Playgroup Movement' by Brenda Crowe, 4th Edn., 1983.

A book intended for primary school teachers is 'Reading in Today's Schools' by Keith Gardner, published by Oliver & Boyd, price £4.95, SBN O 05 003801X. As well as surveying and explaining what is being done in schools, Mr. Gardner "offers lucid guidelines for those who have difficulty in balancing the claims and strengths of apparently 'rival' approaches."

The case for 'real' books is argued by Liz Waterland in her book, 'Read with me', SBN O 903355, price £2.35, post free, from the Thimble Press, Lockwood, Station Road, South Woodchester, Stroud, GL5 5EQ.

The Centre for Children's Books, 45 East Hill, London, SW18 2QZ, sells books about children's literature for parents and teachers by mail order. For details send a large S.A.E. to the Centre.

For teachers and others with a professional interest in education the United Kingdom Reading Association publishes two journals, 'Reading' and the 'Journal of Research in Reading'. Details can be obtained from the Administrative Secretary, U.K.R.A., c/o Edge Hill College, St. Helens Road, Ormskirk, Lancs. L39 4QP.

Mums and Dads with an insatiable thirst for knowledge may get ideas for further reading from the bibliography, 'Involving parents in the teaching of reading : some key sources', price £2 including postage, and obtainable from the Publications Department, Division of Education, University of Sheffield, Arts Tower, Sheffield, S10 2TN. Over one hundred publications are listed together with descriptive notes.

APPENDIX

More books for Parents

Achieving Literacy. Margaret Meek. Routledge, Kegan Paul. £6.95.

Learning to Read. Margaret Meek. Bodley Head. £5.95 SBN O 370 30722 4

Reading Through Play. Carol Baker. Macdonald Education.

The Helen Oxenbury Nursery Story Book, Heinemann. £6.95. SBN434 95602 3

Teaching Your Down's Syndrome Infant, Marci Hanson. MPT Press Ltd., Falcon House, Cable Street, Lancaster

The Nursery Story Book. Kay Choras. Collins. £5.95 SBN 00 195246 3.

Learning to Read with Picture Books. Jill Bennett. Signal £2.40 SBN 0 903355 18 3.

Reaching Out. Stories for Readers of 6 - 8 J Bennett. Signal £1.50 SBN 0 903355 06 X

Babies Need Books. Dorothy Butler. Penguin. £2.25

Read with me. Dorothy Butler. Penguin. £2.35.

Success and failure in learning to read. Ronald Morris. Penguin. £1.95.

Running a Mother and Toddler Club. Joyce Donoghue. Allen & Unwin.

Book Selection Guides.

The Read Aloud Handbook, Jim Trelease, Penguin. £2.50.

British Book News - Children's Books. Published by
the British Council, quarterly, Sub: £12.50
p.a.,distributed by Basil Blackwell, 108, Cowley
Road, Oxford, OX4 1JF.

School Librarian, quarterly £20 p.a., Published by
the School Library Association, 29 George Street,
Oxford, OX1 2AY.

Reading for Enjoyment 0-6. Dorothy Butler, Baker
Book Services. 95p.

Reading for Enjoyment 7-11. Dorothy Butler,
Baker Book Services. 95p

Books for Keeps. Published by the School Bookshop
Association, 1 Effingham Road, Lee, London SE12.
Bi-monthly, £6.30 p.a.

Books for Your Children. Three times a year, £3.50
p.a. from Mrs. A. Wood, P.O. Box 507, Harborne,
Birmingham, B17 8PJ.

Children's Books in Print. Annual. £21. J. Whitaker
& Sons Ltd., 12 Dyott Street, London, WC1A 1DF.

Children's Book News. Quarterly, £3.00 p.a.
Published by Baker Book Services, Little Mead,
Alfold Road, Cranleigh, Surrey, GU6 5NU.

Children's Books of the Year, 1985. National Book
League. £3.50 SBN O 85353 395 4

Good Book Guide to Children's Books. Penguin,.

N.B. Most children's libraries will allow
parents to consult the above publications although
they will not usually be available for loan.

Books for Children

Any list of this type soon becomes out-of-date.
There is a huge output of children's books, and many
are soon out-of-print. Nevertheless, a few, recently

published books for pre-readers and early readers are mentioned below:-

For under threes:-
What happens next. Bill Gillham. Methuen.
Where is Bobo? Bill Gillham. Methuen.
For three to five year olds:-
The Very Hungry Caterpillar. Eric Carle. Hamish Hamilton.
Where's My Hat? Morris. Hodder & Stoughton.
The Tiger Who Came to Tea. Judith Kerr. Picture Puffin.
Bears in the Night. Berenstain. Collins.

Publications for Teachers

Working Together: Parents and Professionals as Partners. £2.75
Parent involvement: What does it mean and how do we achieve it? £2.75.
Reading: Parents, Children and Teaching. £2.40
Obtainable from the National Children's Bureau, 8 Wakley Street, London EC1V 7QE.
Reading. Frank Smith. Cambridge University Press. £4.95.

Some Reading Schemes in Print, 1986

TITLE   *PUBLISHER*

One, Two three and away Wm. Collins, Sons & Co. Ltd., 8 Grafton Street, London, W1X 3LA

TITLE	PUBLISHER
Breakthrough to Literacy	Longman Group Ltd., Burnt Mill,Harlow, Essex CM20 2JE
Dominoes	Oliver & Boyd, 1 Baxter's Place, Leith Walk, Edinburgh, EH1 3BB
Sparks	Blackie & Son, Ltd., Bishopbriggs, Glasgow, G64 2NZ
Link Up	Holmes McDougall Ltd. 137 Leith Walk, Edinburgh, EH6 8NS
Language in Action	Macmillan Education Ltd. Houndmills, Basingstoke, Hants, RG21 2XS
Reading 360	Ginn & Co. Ltd., Prebendal House, Parson's Fee, Aylesbury, Bucks, HP20 2QZ
Crown	Arnold-Wheaton, Parkside Lane, Leeds, LS11 5TD
Language Patterns	Holt, Rinehart & Winston, St. Anne's Road, Eastbourne, East Sussex, BN21 3UN
Storychest	E.J. Arnold & Son Ltd., Parkside Lane, Leeds, LS11 5TD

TITLE	PUBLISHER
3L (Language, Literature, Literacy)	Reading Development Resources, 1 Redington Gardens, Hampstead, London ,NW3 7RT
Journeys to Reading	Schofield & Sims, Dogley Mill, Fenay Bridge, Huddersfield, HD8 0NQ
Oxford Reading Tree	Oxford University Press, Walton Street, Oxford, OX2 6DP
Puddle Lane	Ladybird Books Ltd., P.O. Box 12, Beeches Road, Loughborough, Leics, LE11 2NQ
Open Door	Thomas Nelson & Sons Ltd., Mayfield Road, Walton-on-Thames, Surrey, KT12 5PL

Mail Order Suppliers of Educational Materials

Early Learning	Hawksworth, Swindon, SN2 1TT
ESA International Ltd.,	Esavian Works, Fairview Road, Stevenage, Herts, SG1 2NX

James Galt & Co. Ltd.,	Brookfield Road, Cheadle, Cheshire, SK9 2PF
Hestair Hope Ltd.,	St. Philip's Drive, Royton, Oldham, OL2 6AG
Webucational	P.O. Box 81 ,Wimborne, Dorset, BH21 3UT
LDA	Duke Street, Wisbech, Cambs, PE13 2AE
Taskmaster	Morris Road, Leicester, LE2 6BR
Playplus	18 Hazeldene Drive, Pinner, Middx., HA5 3NJ
Four to Eight	Medway House, Faircham Industrial Estate, Evelyn Drive, Leicester, LE3 2BU

N.B. Some suppliers add handling charges for small orders, or stipulate minimum amounts below which they will not supply customers. Parents may overcome this difficulty by co-operating and clubbing together to assemble a larger order.

Mail Order Suppliers of Educational Books

Able Children Ltd	Caxtons, Park Lane, Knebworth, Herts., SG3 6PF
Books for Children	Farndon Road, Market Harborough, Leics., LE16 9NR

Bookworm Club	Napier Place, Cumbernauld, Glasgow, G68 0DN
Gifted Children's Information Centre	21 Hampton Lane, Solihull, B91 2QJ
Letterbox Library,	1st Floor, 5 Bradbury Street, London, N16 8JN (Concentrates on books challenging accepted stereotypes)
Macdonald 3/4/5	Purnell Books, Paulton, Bristol, BS18 5BR
Puffin Club,	Penguin Books, Bath Road, Harmondsworth, Middlesex ,UB7 0DA (Quarterly magazines for children)
Red House Books	Industrial Estate, Station Road, Witney, OX8 6YQ
The Good Book Guide	91 Great Russell Street, London, WC1
Usborne Books at Home	221a Banbury Road, Oxford, OX2 7HQ
Offspring, E.J. Arnold	Butterley Street, Leeds, LS10 1AX

Organisations Concerned with Education

Advisory Centre for Education, 18 Victoria Park
Square, London, E2 9PB
Association for All Speech Impaired Children,
347 Central Markets, London, EC1A 9NH

British Association for Early Childhood Education,
Montgomery Hall, Kennington Oval, London,
SE11 5SW
British Dyslexia Association, Church Lane,
Peppard, Oxon, RJ9 5JN
Community Education Development Centre, Briton
Road, Coventry, CV2 4LF
Down's Children Association,
Quinborne Community Centre, Ridgacre Road,
Birmingham, B32 2TW

Home and School Council,
Sec: Mrs B Bullivant, 81 Rusllings Road,
Sheffield, S11 7AB
Independent Schools Information Service,
26 Caxton Street, London, SW1H 0RG
Invalid Children's Aid Association,
126 Buckingham Palace Road, London
SW1 9SN
National Association for Gifted Children,
1 South Audley Street, London W1Y 5DQ
National Association for Maternal and Child Welfare,
1 South Audley Street, London WIY 5DQ
National Association for Mentally Handicapped
Children,119-123 Golden Lane, London, EC1Y 0RT
National Association for the Teaching of English,
49 Broomgrove Road, Sheffield, S10 2NA
National Association for the Welfare of Children in
Hospital,
77 Exton Street, London, SE1
National Association for Remedial Education ,
2 Lichfield Road, Stafford, ST17 4JX

National Children's Bureau,
8 Wakely Street, London ,EC1V 7QE
National Christian Education Council,
Robert Denholm House, Nutfield, Redhill,
RH1 4HW
National Council for One Parent Families,
255 Kentish Town Road, London NW5
National Confederation of Parent-Teacher
Associations,
43 Stonebridge Road, Northfleet, Gravesend, Kent,
DA11 9DS

National Deaf Children's Society,
45 Hereford Road, London ,W2 5AG
National Froebel Foundation,
Grove House, Roehampton Lane, London, SW15
5PJ
National Library for the Handicapped Child,
Lynton House, Tavistock Square,London, WC1H
9LT
National Elfrida Rathbone Society, 11 Whitworth
Street, Manchester
National Society for Autistic Children ,
1a Golders Green Road, London ,NW11 8EA
Pre-School Playgroups Association,
Alford House, Aveline Street, London
SE11 5 DH
Royal National Institute for the Deaf,
105 Gower Street, London, WC1E 6AH
Scottish Pre-School Playgroups Association,
7 Royal Terrace, Glasgow, G3 7NT
Society for Italic Handwriting,
69 Arlington Road, London, NW1 7ES

The Children's Society,
Old Town Hall, Kennington Road,
London, SE11 4QD
The Mother's Union,
24 Tufton Street, London, SW1P 3RB
United Kingdom Reading Association,
c/o Edge Hill College, St. Helens Road,
Ormskirk, Lancs., L39 4QP
World-wide Education Service of the PNEU,
44-50 Osnaburgh Street, London, NW1 3NN
Royal Association for Disability & Rehabilitation
(RADAR),
25 Mortimer Street, London , W1N 8AB